FOOTBALL

FOOTBALL: THE OFFENSE

BRYANT LLOYD

The Rourke Book Co., Inc.
Vero Beach, Florida 32964

EDITORIAL SERVICES:
Penworthy Learning Systems

Library of Congress Cataloging-in-Publication Data

Lloyd, Bryant. 1942
    Football: the offense / by Bryant Lloyd.
        p. cm. — (Football)
    Includes index
    Summary: Discusses the basics in football offense, covering such aspects as formations and the work of the center, the quarterback, the wide receivers, and the ends.
        ISBN 1-55916-213-9 (alk. paper)
        1. Football—Offense—Juvenile literature. [1. Football.]
    I. Title II. Series
    GV950.7.L56 1997
    796.332'2—dc21   97–765
                                                                CIP
                                                                AC

Printed in the USA

TABLE OF CONTENTS

FOOTBALL OFFENSE

A team wins a football game by scoring more points than the other team, its opponent. The team's **offense** (AW fents) scores most of its points.

The offense is the part of a team that controls the football. The job of the offense is to control the ball until it can score. The offense runs or throws the football against the **defense** (DEE fents) of the opponent.

The draw is a common play used by offenses. The quarterback steps back as if to pass. Instead, he hands the ball to a running back. The defenders, meanwhile, have been drawn to the quarterback, opening the line for the runner.

The offense puts the football into play and tries to move it forward against the defense.

CONTROLLING THE OFFENSE

All football games are played for a set number of minutes. The longer an offense can keep the football, the less time its opponent has the ball. The offense keeps the football by earning new sets of **downs** (DOUNZ), or plays.

By advancing the football, the offense can earn a new set of downs.

The offense gathers in a huddle to call its next play.

If the offense gains 10 yards (9 meters) in four or fewer downs, it is given another set of four downs. It continues to earn new sets of downs until it scores or turns the ball over to the opponent.

FORMATIONS

The 11 members of a football offense set themselves in certain positions before a play begins. The arrangement of the players is called a **formation** (fawr MAY shun). Football has a huge variety of formations.

The offense must have seven players along the **line of scrimmage** (LYN UV SKRIM idj), which is where the ball lies on the field. It has four players in the backfield behind the line.

Each formation is used for a special purpose. Each person in the formation plays a position, such as center.

A typical offensive formation in position against the defense.

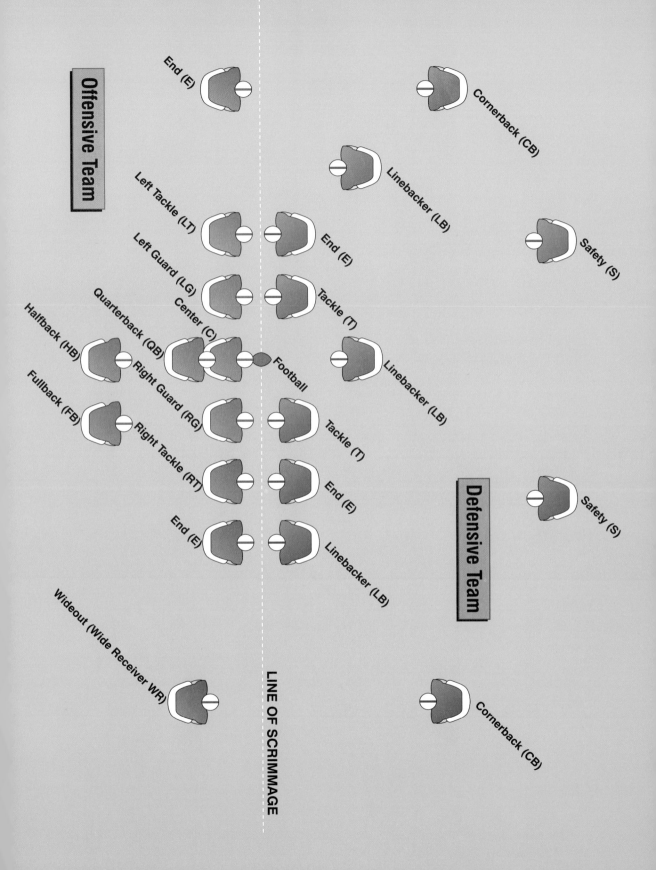

THE CENTER

Part of the center's job is to **snap** (SNAP) the football. Snap means the center lifts the football to a teammate, usually the quarterback. Sometimes the center must hike the ball backward, between his legs, 7 or 8 yards (just over 7 meters). The center's snap begins most plays in a football game.

The quarterback lets the center know when to snap the ball by counting aloud. The center must always remember the snap number. He must also be a tough, strong blocker.

During the 1880's, a former Yale University football player, Walter Camp, helped make important changes in the rules. He began the use of downs and the snap from center to quarterback.

Green team's center snaps the football
back into the hands of the quarterback.

THE QUARTERBACK

The quarterback leads the offense. He is the general on the field. The quarterback tells his teammates the next play as they huddle between plays.

The quarterback lines up behind the center in the backfield. In most formations, the quarterback takes the snap right from the center's hands.

The quarterback calls numbers. The center snaps the ball backward on a number decided in the huddle.

The quarterback cocks his arm to throw a forward pass.

A quarterback must be smart and highly skilled. He handles the ball on almost every offensive play. He may pass the football or run with it. He may pitch the ball underhanded or hand it to a running back.

RUNNING BACKS

Running backs set up in the backfield, usually behind and to one side of the quarterback.

Running backs either **block** (BLAHK), carry the football, or catch passes. Halfbacks and tailbacks are usually used more often for running than blocking. A fullback, on the other hand, usually blocks more than he runs. Most formations have one or two running backs in addition to the quarterback.

Running backs are among the fastest and most skilled football players.

Many football victories are called "upsets." An upset is a win by a team that most people expected to lose the game!

Running back carries football in hand farther from the nearest ball tackler.

WIDEOUTS

Wideouts, also known as flankers or wide receivers, are pass catchers. They set up in the offensive backfield, wide to the left or right of the quarterback.

Wideouts are fast and skilled receivers. They have what coaches call "good hands." They can catch and hold a football even among many defenders.

The speed of wideouts helps them escape tacklers.

Good wideout watches ball, not tackler, as he prepares to make a catch.

ENDS

Offensive ends line up along the line of scrimmage. Ends are usually the last offensive players along the line.

Ends are used mostly for blocking. They help protect their quarterback if he is passing the football. Their blocks also help keep defenders away from the ball carrier.

Offensive end (far right) is usually a blocker, but he can be a pass catcher, too.

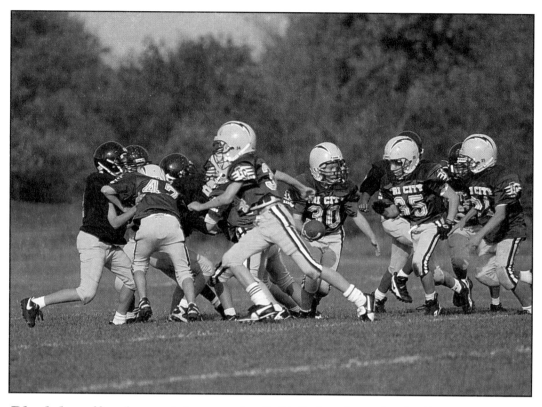

Block by offensive end (green, far left) helps free the ball carrier to run around the end position.

Ends are usually tall, and they are faster than other linemen. Ends with good hands are often used as pass receivers.

LINEMEN

Besides the center and ends, the offense has linemen called guards and tackles. The guards and tackles are blockers. In most formations, they do not catch the football or run with it.

These linemen are big and strong. They must protect the quarterback and open paths, called holes, among the defensive players with their block. The holes allow the offense's ball carrier to run past tacklers.

About 20 bowl games are played after college football's regular season ends. The oldest of them is the Rose Bowl, first played in 1902. The Rose Bowl is in Pasadena, California.

Offensive lineman (yellow, far right) blocks charge of defensive lineman.

GLOSSARY

block (BLAHK) — physical contact made by an offensive player to stop the progress of a defensive player; the act of making contact to stop or slow a defensive player

defense (DEE fents) — the team that is protecting its goal line against the team with the football

down (DOUN) — any one of the plays run by a football team from the line of scrimmage

formation (fawr MAY shun) — any one of the many ways in which a football team arranges its players in offensive positions

line of scrimmage (LYN UV SKRIM idj) — an imaginary line across a football field; place where the ball is put after a play

offense (AW fents) — the team with the ball; the team that puts a football into play

snap (SNAP) — the movement of the football by the center to another player

Teamwork helps make an offense go. Here the quarterback hands the football to a running back. His linemen will try to make a path for him.

INDEX